Published by
PRI Publishing (Professional Research Institute Publishing)
P.O. Box 74
Clifford, VA 24533
Tel: (434) 263-8256, Fax: (434) 263-5797

In association with Prodigy Development Foundation

Library of Congress Cataloging-in-Publication Data

Bernardini, Robert.
The Golfer's Night Be-*FORE!* Christmas / written by Robert Bernardini; Illustrated by Janice Donato. - 1st ed.
p. cm.
LCCN 2003096888
ISBN 0-9703269-7-1

1. Christmas--Poetry. 2. Santa Claus--Poetry. 3. Golf--Poetry.
I. Donato, Janice Poltrick. II. Moore, Clement Clarke, 1779-1863.
III. Title.

PF3552.E72745G65 2003   811/.54
QBI33-1629

Printed and bound in Korea

The Golfer's

Night
Be F○re!
Christmas

Written by
Robert Bernardini

Illustrated by
Janice Donato

'Twas the night beFore! Christmas
And out on the links,
Not a birdie was stirring,
Not a putt there to sink.

My golf bag was hung
By the chimney with care,
A new set of irons
Was my wish for this year.

And I in my plus fours
And Ben Hogan cap,
Had decided to lay-up
For a long winter's nap.

My wife, she was laughing,
My dog looked chagrined.
But I swore this year
The club title I'd win.

So I started to visualize
As the pros say to do -
Long drives and stiff irons
And a hole-in-one too!

But just as my mind
Had slipped into the "zone",
There came from the rooftop
A long painful moan!

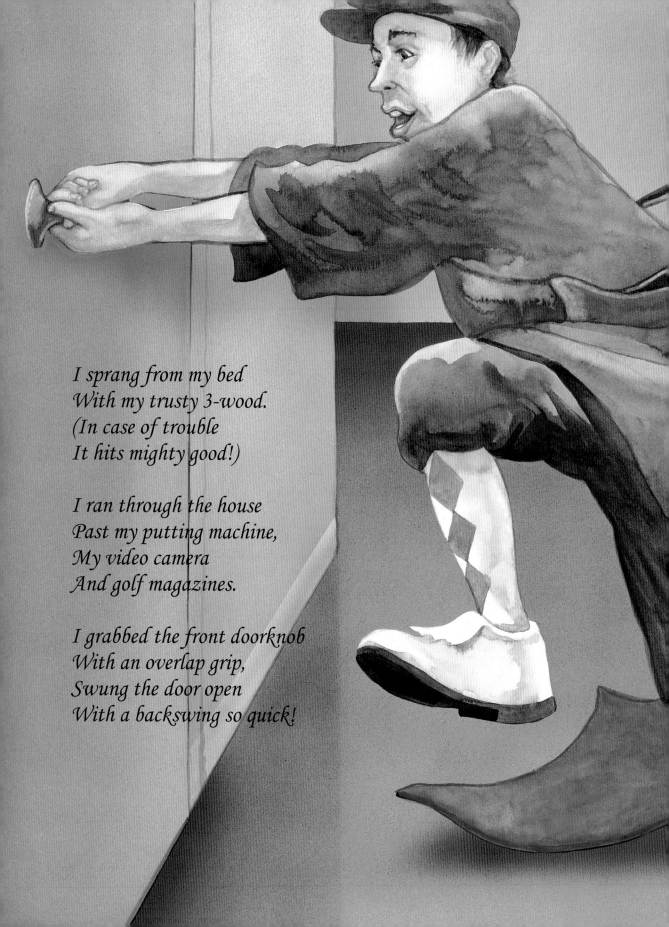

I sprang from my bed
With my trusty 3-wood.
(In case of trouble
It hits mighty good!)

I ran through the house
Past my putting machine,
My video camera
And golf magazines.

I grabbed the front doorknob
With an overlap grip,
Swung the door open
With a backswing so quick!

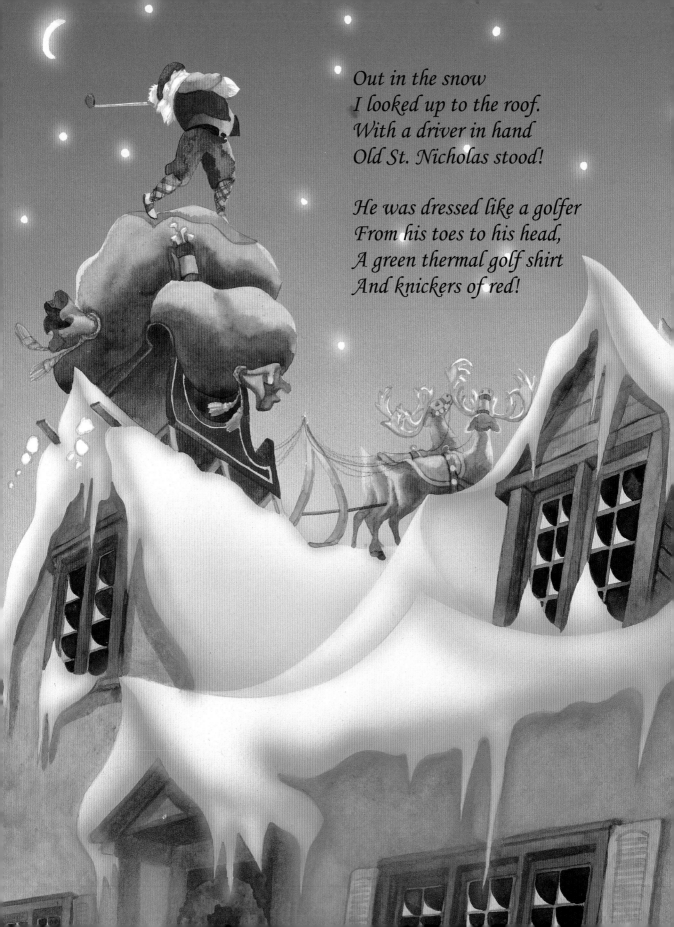

Out in the snow
I looked up to the roof.
With a driver in hand
Old St. Nicholas stood!

He was dressed like a golfer
From his toes to his head,
A green thermal golf shirt
And knickers of red!

A plaid Scottish hat
And some new soft spike shoes,
Made it hard to believe
Any match he could lose!

His grip, it was Vardon,
His stance slightly closed.
A driving mat perched
On the sleigh whence he rose...

A grimace of pain
Was carved into his face.
As deep as a divot...
(That you should replace!)

"Oh %&*# and *%#@,"
I heard Santa swear!
"Gosh-dang-it, Rudolph,
It just isn't fair!

"With all of my magic
I can't hit it straight!
A hook or a slice
Or a shank is my fate!"

He swung again hard
And hit a big slice,
And muttered again
As the ball curved in flight.

"I know how you feel,"
I yelled up to St. Nick.
"But I have a tip
That might fix that slice quick!"

He looked down at me
With a tear in his eye,
And before I knew it
I started to fly!

Up to the rooftop
I floated real slow,
Like a delicate lob-shot
Hit by a pro.

Santa winked at me
And gave me an iron,
Out of the golf bag
That stood there beside him.

"Show me," he said,
As I gathered myself.
"I dare say I'm stymied,
And boy, I need help!"

"You see," I said, "Santa,
It's all in the wrists.
You're cocking too soon,
And that gives you fits.

"And keep your head steady,
You don't want to sway.
That belly of yours sometimes
Gets in the way."

"Umph," Santa coughed
As he teed up a ball.
"Widen your stance," I said,
"Stand loose and tall."

His backswing was slower,
His wrists cocked a little...
And this time he nailed that ball
Straight down the middle!

We both watched that silver ball
Climb through the night.
Up 'mongst the stars,
No prettier sight!

It hung there so long
As if frozen in space,
Like a new twinkling star
Had just fallen in place!

"You see," Santa grinned,
"You now know the truth...
Stars are just golf balls
I've hit from the roof!

"The Dippers, Orion,
The whole Milky Way,
Are golf balls I've hit
When it's golf that I play!"

I stood there amazed
Watching this jolly elf,
Launch shooting stars
"Ho-ho-ho-ing" himself!

"Partner," he said,
"You are right, I am sure!
My nasty weak slice
You have finally cured!"

He smiled a smile
Only golfers would know,
Then floated me down
From the rooftop so slow.

"I'm late for my tee-time,
I must fly off, but
Maybe next year
You can teach me to putt!"

He climbed in the sleigh
And took hold of the reins,
And called to the reindeer
True golfing nicknames...

"On Eagle, on Longball,
On Chipshot and Bogey!
On Divot, on Sandtrap,
On Backspin and Birdie!"

Then as he flew off
And tipped me his cap,
I swear I could hear
The gallery clap!

And I heard him call out
As he swung back around,
"Merry Christmas FORE! all,
And FORE! all, a good round!"

Safety First Please! And it Won't Make You Sneeze!
The Complete Children's Safety Kit

THE COMPLETE "SAFETY FIRST PLEASE" KIT

"The Most Complete Program for Children's Protection Available."

Did you realize that according to FBI statistics, every 41 seconds another child disappears? Abductions, kidnappings, and getting lost are real dangers for kids these days! Even worse, every year 6,700 children die and another 50,000 are seriously injured because of accidents and every day mishaps!

Protect your child to the fullest with the most gentle, effective, fun, and doctor approved methods that ensure your child's safety. The *Safety First Please Protection Kit* uses a unique 'multi-modal' approach to teaching your child how to recognize dangerous situations and avoid them. For ages 3-12. Each kit includes:

- Critically acclaimed full color children's book *Safety First Please* (8½ x 11 hardcover)
- CD (or tape) with safety songs, book narration, and sound tracks
- Fingerprinting kit
- DNA sample kit
- Dental chart
- Folder for recent photo, personal/medical information, and important phone numbers
- Twenty-four *I'm a Safety Seal Kid* stickers – kids love them!
- Plush beany toy of *Sterling the Safety Seal*
- Teachers/Parents Instruction and Resource Manual

$29.95 + $5 S&H / Book only–$15.95 + $5 S&H / Book & CD only – $19.95 + $5 S&H

"As a child psychiatrist, I am always interested in new ways to help children be safe. The Safety First Please Kit is an excellent program that covers a lot of very important issues that all come down to keeping our children safe. I like the way it asks children what they would do… Using a multi-modal approach of reading, hearing, seeing, singing, rhyming, etc. will help this information 'sink in' and avoids the 'fear factor.' Thanks for your efforts."

— J Ronald Hell, M.D.

The Crystal and the Keyhole and Santa's Magic Secret

What child hasn't wondered how the presents get under the tree if there is no chimney for Santa? Well, little Jackie is no different and he's determined to find out! While waiting under the Christmas tree on Christmas Eve, he's surprised by a bright rainbow of light that explodes through the keyhole of his front door. Two cute and ambitious elves, Katie and Ben, grow out of the light and commence putting presents under the tree. Jackie befriends them, and learns that with the help of their magic crystal, they can get into houses that Santa cannot... "When there is no chimney, we elves save the day!" ...and Santa is up on the roof waiting for his elves to return from doing their job.

When they get ready to leave, Katie pulls out the magic crystal, and she and Ben say the magic words... "And together they said three times in a hush, Merry Christmas to all, and to all peace and love." Magic ensues, as Jackie watches and learns the whole secret about the elves, Santa Claus and Christmas without a chimney.

This heart-warming tale will enchant young and old alike with its sincere message, brilliant illustrations and surprising ending. And it will finally answer your youngsters' questions about how the presents are delivered when there is no chimney! 8½" x 11" full color hardcover.

$15.95 + $5 S&H

Sneak Preview — Coming in October, 2003 from PRI Publishing
The Golfer's Night BeFORE! Christmas

The Christmas story every golfer has been waiting for is finally here! *The Golfer's Night BeFORE! Christmas* reveals the truth about Santa's love for the game of golf – and a problem with his golf swing! Dressed in red knickers, green thermal golf shirt and golf shoes, Santa pauses on his rounds to hit a few practice shots off of a fellow golf enthusiast's roof. But there's a problem! Santa just can't stop hitting a slice! His new golfing buddy comes to his rescue by offering a few tips and giving Santa a golf lesson right there on the roof on Christmas Eve! He tells Santa, "And keep your head steady, you don't want to sway... That belly of yours sometimes gets in the way!" Soon, Santa gets in the groove... "His backswing was slower, his wrists cocked a little... And this time he nailed that ball

straight down the middle!"

Filled with golf language, traditions, humor, and class, this book will make every golfer smile and rejoice in golfing satisfaction. You will not only see Santa's jolly golf swing, but also learn the amazing and magical secret of where his golf balls end up after he hits them off the roof.

The Par-fect gift and stocking-stuffer for any golfer on your Christmas list! Be a good caddy and get *The Golfer's Night BeFORE! Christmas* for the golfer you love!

"And I heard him call out as he swung back around... Merry Christmas FORE! all and FORE! all a good round!"
7" x 10" full color hardcover.

$11.95 + $5 S&H

PRI Publishing   P.O. Box 74, Clifford, VA 24533   Phone: (434) 263-8256   Fax: (434) 263-5797   email proreach@aol.com
Distributor & Bookstore discounts available.

PRI Publishing

1047 Falling Rock Drive,
Amherst, VA 24521
(434) 263-8256, Fax: (434) 263-5797
Email: proreach@aol.com

Order Form

Item	Price/Items	Number of Items	S&H	Total .
Safety First Please! Complete Safety Kit	$29.95			
Safety First Please! Book Only	$15.95			
The Truth About Children's Health	$19.95			
The Crystal & the Keyhole – Santa's Magic Secret	$15.95			
The Golfer's Night Be-FORE! Christmas	$11.95			

(Virginia Residents add 4.5% sales tax)   **TOTAL** _____

Shipping Charges:
1-3 books = $5   3-5 books = $7   5-10 books = $10   11 or more books = $1 each
Shipping Charges for *Safety First Please Complete Safety Kit*:
1 kit = $5   2-4 kits = $7   5 or more kits = $2 each

Mail Order to and make check or money order payable to:
PRI Publishing
1047 Falling Rock Drive,
Amherst, VA 24521
24 Hour Order Line:
(434) 263-8256
24 Hour Fax:
(434) 263-5797
email: proreach@aol.com

Ship to: Name_____
Address_____
City_____State_____Zip_____

MasterCard & Visa only *(We **do not** take AMEX or Discover)*

Account Number: _____ Expir. Date_____

Signature_____